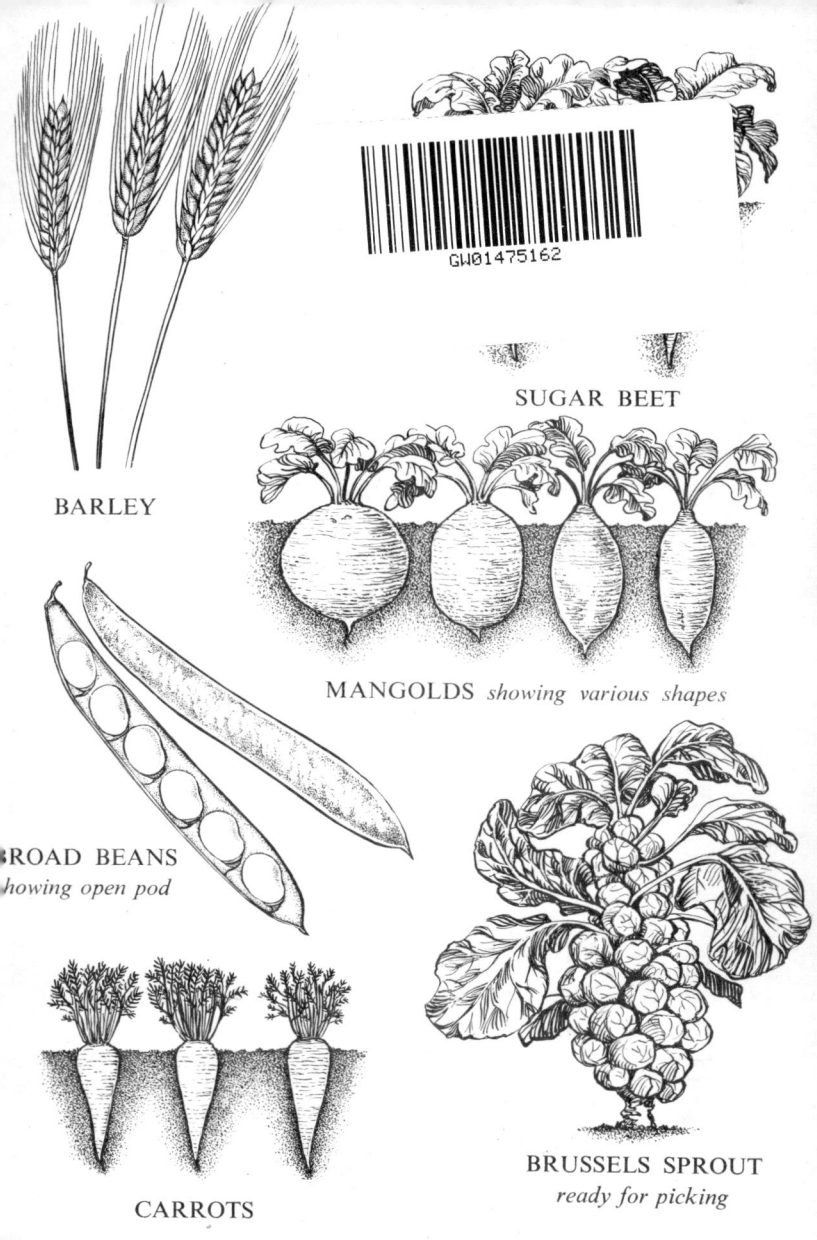

Series 606B

This is another carefully planned Ladybird book in the 'People at Work' section.

A relatively simple vocabulary, large, clear type and superb illustrations are used to give interesting and accurate information about farmers and farming. It shows how the land is prepared and the various crops that are harvested, the animals that are reared and the modern machinery that helps farmers to produce our food. It is a book that will help to answer many of the questions that lively children ask.

A LADYBIRD
'EASY-READING'
BOOK

NET

A LADYBIRD 'EASY-READING' BOOK

'People at Work'
THE FARMER

by
I. & J. HAVENHAND

with illustrations by
JOHN BERRY

Publishers: Wills & Hepworth Ltd., Loughborough
First published 1963 *Printed in England*

THE FARMER

All farmers are very busy men, but they are not all busy doing the same kind of work.

A long time ago all farms were worked in the same way. They were called mixed-farms. The farmer grew some crops and kept some animals.

To-day some farmers still run mixed-farms, but others run their farms in a special way.

Stock farmers buy very good animals and just rear cows or sheep or pigs. Other farmers spend all their time growing crops. They are all farmers, whatever they grow or rear.

The farmer who tills the land and gets crops from it is called an arable farmer.

He grows corn crops like wheat, barley and oats. The wheat is made into flour, breakfast foods and animal food. Barley is used by brewers to make beer and is also made into animal food. Oats are made into porridge and animal food.

The arable farmer grows root crops like potatoes, sugar-beet, turnips and mangolds. He grows other vegetable crops for green-grocers to sell, for canning factories to can, and for animal food.

The arable farmer must get the land ready, sow the seeds, tend the young plants and harvest the crop.

First of all the farmer ploughs the land. He pulls the plough behind a tractor. The plough usually has three plough-shares, and these cut into the soil and turn it over. The cuts are called furrows. All farmers like to plough good, straight furrows.

When the fields are ploughed, the frost, the wind, the sun and the rain all help to break up the soil.

The farmer in the picture is using a cultivator to break up the lumps of soil. Then he uses a harrow to level the soil and make a fine tilth.

One kind of harrow has a zig-zag metal frame with short metal spikes which stick into the ground. A set of three of these harrows can be pulled behind a tractor.

Another kind of harrow is a disc-harrow. This has many sharp-edged discs like wheels. These cut-up heavy soil.

When the soil has been harrowed, it is ready for the seed to be sown.

Long ago farmers had to scatter seed by hand. To-day a machine called a seed-drill is used. This is a long box on wheels, with pipes leading down to the soil.

The farmer tows the seed-drill behind a tractor, and sets the seeds in neat rows. The farmer in the picture is dragging a spiked harrow behind the seed-drill to cover the seeds with soil.

When the young plants are growing, the farmer sprays them to kill the weeds and pests. This helps to grow better crops.

The hay-harvest is the beginning of a very busy time on many farms.

To cut the grass a mowing-machine is towed behind a tractor. Some farmers cut the grass when it is young, and press it down in a pit. Then they add molasses, a sort of black treacle, and this helps to make silage. Silage is a very good winter food for cows.

Other farmers leave the grass in the fields to dry. Dry grass is called hay, and is a useful winter food for animals.

Most farmers use baling machines to pick up the hay. The baling machine moves up and down the field, picking up the hay, and at the same time pressing and tying it into neat bales. Then the bales are loaded on to a trailer, and are taken away to be stacked in barns ready for the winter.

Dried corn stems, called straw, can also be picked up by this machine, and pressed and baled in the same way. The straw is also stored by the farmer, and is used as bedding for animals.

A few years ago the farmer needed several machines, many men, and a lot of time to harvest his corn.

The corn was cut and tied into sheaves by a reaper-binder. These sheaves were put into piles called stooks, and left to dry. When the corn sheaves were dry they were taken and stacked near the farm.

Later in the year the corn was passed through a machine called a threshing machine. The threshing machine separated the grains of corn from the straw, and from their outer coverings, called chaff.

To-day the farmer has one machine to harvest his corn. This machine is called a combine-harvester. It cuts and threshes the corn.

The combine-harvester is a large machine which may be driven and worked by one man. At the front of the machine are flails, or arms, which draw the corn on to the cutters. The corn then passes up a moving belt into the box-like body of the machine.

The threshing is done inside the combine-harvester, which separates the corn into straw, chaff and grain.

The threshing is done as the harvester moves along. The chaff and the straw fall from the machine on to the ground.

Some smaller combine-harvesters pour the grain into sacks. These sacks are held ready by one or two men. When they are full the sacks are tied and dropped in the field, and are then collected by a tractor and trailer.

Large harvesters store the grain in a bin until a box-trailer comes alongside. Then the grain is allowed to flow from the bin into the box-trailer.

The farmer who keeps animals must also grow those crops which help to feed them in the winter. He grows beans, mangolds, turnips and swedes, beet and kale. All these are good food for animals.

Farmers also grow crops for us to eat. They grow fields of potatoes, and have special machines for planting them—and lifting them out of the ground. In the picture you will see a machine which lifts the potatoes out of the ground, and leaves them on the surface to be collected.

Fields of peas, sprouts and cabbages are also planted.

Some farmers grow sugar beet. When the farmer lifts the sugar beet he cuts off the plant tops. After these tops have wilted, they are good food for cattle. The sugar beet is taken to the factory and sugar is made from it.

In some parts of the country farmers grow hops. The hop fields have high hedges around them to break the wind. The farmers put up tall posts in the fields and stretch wires on them. The hops grow up the wires. Hops are used to make beer.

Dairy farmers keep herds of cows. These are kept mainly for the milk they give, and not so much for their meat.

Dairy cows like Jerseys, Friesians and Ayrshires are lean-looking cows with big bones. The farmer can get up to six or seven gallons a day from a good milking cow. Jersey cows give less milk, but it is more creamy.

The more milk a cow gives, the more water it must drink. A cow will drink up to ten gallons of water a day.

At one time cows were milked by hand. The farmer sat on his three legged stool by the side of each cow and milked it. He could only milk one cow at a time, so milking filled a large part of his day.

To-day on most farms the cows are milked by a milking machine. Twice a day at milking time the cows are led to the milking shed. This shed is kept very clean. The walls are often tiled and the concrete floor is washed every day.

The dairy farmer has to see that everything he uses for milking is very clean. The milking machinery, the milk cooler and the churns are cleaned with boiling water or steam. All cows are tested to see that they are in good health. This means that the milk is pure and fit for us to drink.

On a large dairy farm the farmer has a cowman who looks after the herd. At milking times he opens the milking shed doors and each cow walks to its own stall.

The cowman washes the sides of the cow and its udder. Rubber cups are fixed to the teats of the cow's udder, and the milking machine is started. This sucks the milk from the cow through pipes. The milk is then passed over the cooler and into churns.

The churns are put near the farm gate to be collected by the lorry from the dairy company. At large dairies the milk is bottled, or made into cheese or butter. Some of the milk is dried and made into milk powder.

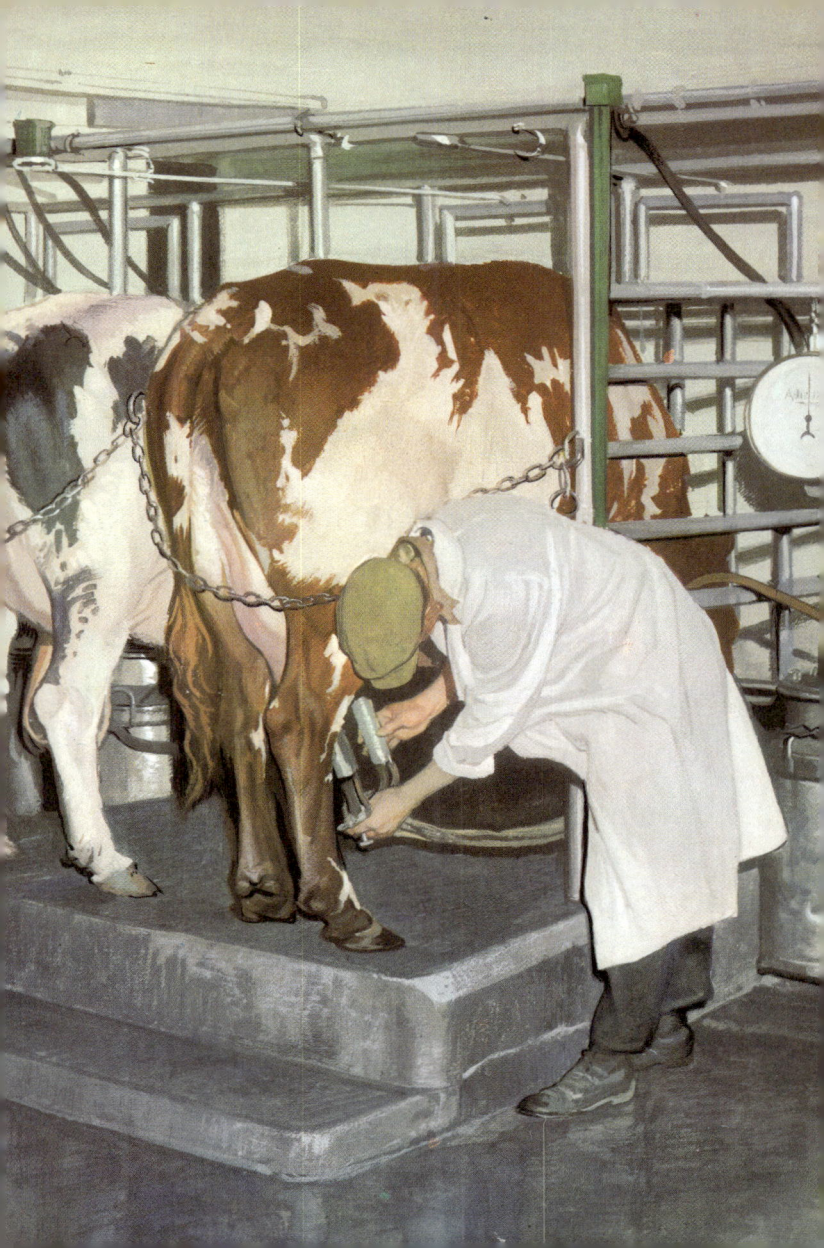

Some farmers are stock farmers. They keep cows and bullocks for their beef. Good beef animals like Shorthorns, Herefords and Aberdeen Angus are not as bony as dairy cows.

Usually these farmers buy bull-calves from dairy farmers who only wish to keep cows. After these calves have been fattened for about two years, they are then sold to a butcher.

Some farmers keep Friesian and Shorthorn cows. These are very useful cows as they are good milkers and can also be sold for beef.

Sheep farmers in this country keep sheep mainly for the purpose of breeding lambs. These lambs are later sold for meat.

The female sheep are called ewes, and each ewe has one or two lambs each year.

These farmers often live in hilly districts. There the land is too difficult to farm in any other way. The sheep can climb the steep slopes, and eat the short grass which they like.

The farmer brings the sheep down from the hills for the winter. Often he sells the lambs to other farmers who fatten them up on lower pastures.

The sheep farmer is busy with his flock all the year round. Sheep easily become ill, and a good shepherd must watch each one carefully. He often has a sheep dog to help him look after the flock.

The lambs are born early in Spring, and the farmer has to spend most of his time with the ewes and lambs. When the lambs are old enough, the farmer has to arrange for them to be injected against disease. Lambs also have their tails shortened. This helps them to keep clean.

Usually sheep and lambs are dipped once a year. The farmer has a deep trough filled with disinfectant. The sheep are driven into a pen near the deep end of the trough. Then they are pushed into the trough one after the other. As they scramble through, a man with a pole pushes the sheep's head under. This makes sure that every part of each sheep has been disinfected.

This dipping helps to keep the sheep free from insects, like the blowfly, which could harm them.

In May or June the weather is warmer and the farmer can begin shearing his sheep. This means that each sheep has its wool, or fleece, cut off. This is done on clean ground, or on a wooden floor, to keep the fleece clean. The fleece is worth more if it is clean.

The farmer uses electric clippers to cut off the fleece. He quickly turns the sheep over and holds it with his knees. A few quick strokes and the fleece comes off in one piece. The sheep runs away looking quite strange and much smaller.

Pig farmers breed and rear pigs. They keep good sows, or mother pigs, and from them they get litters of piglets. The piglets are fed carefully on pigmeal. They are given just enough to help them to grow to the right size. Too much food makes them fat, and most people do not like fat pork and bacon.

When they are big enough the pigs are sold to the butcher for pork, or to the bacon factory to be turned into bacon.

Some farmers keep hens for the eggs they lay. Sometimes the hens live in batteries. These are cages in which the hens live from the age of six months. Other hens may be kept in deep litter. This means that they live in large sheds with plenty of chopped straw on the ground. In batteries and deep litter the hens are kept warm, well fed, and have plenty of light.

Some farmers keep poultry to be eaten as table birds. These birds are called broilers. They are well fed and are ready for the shops in about ten or twelve weeks.

A cattle market is held every week at a town in the farming district. Most farmers sell some of their animals at the market. The animals are put in pens where other farmers can examine them before they buy.

All the things that a farmer wants to buy can be found in the market. He can buy animals, feeding troughs, tools, tractors and even large machines.

Farmers enjoy a day at the market. There they meet other farmers and friends. They talk about their work and their problems, and get all the latest farming news.

ABERDEEN ANGUS BULL
Black hornless beef breed

BRITISH FRIESIAN COW
A dairy breed which originally came from Holland

AYRSHIRE BULL
Cows of this breed are used for dairy purposes